As stones study stones:

WORDS FOR OTHER COMMON RAVENS.

Pieces of poetry, prose and ponderings by

PATRICIA PORIZ

Pat P

As stones study stones
Copyright © 2018 by Patricia Poriz

No part of this publication may be reproduced, distributed, or transmitted in any form or by any means, including photocopying, recording, or other electronic or mechanical methods, without the prior written permission of the author, except in the case of brief quotations embodied in critical reviews and certain other non-commercial uses permitted by copyright law.

Scripture taken from the HOLY BIBLE NEW INTERNATIONAL VERSION © 1973, 1978, 1984 by International Bible Society. Used by permission of Zondervan Publishing House. All rights reserved.

www.patriciaporiz.com

Tellwell Talent
www.tellwell.ca

ISBN
978-1-77370-715-0 (Hardcover)
978-1-77370-714-3 (Paperback)
978-0-2288-0212-9 (eBook)

For Jim, my favourite person on earth. You coax, cheer and cherish me, and I am always amazed at your steadfastness and humour. You are the binding stone that holds our family together, and you are so loved, from now till eternity.

And for our children and grandchildren, Jesse & Stephanie, Jayne & Jeremy, James & Stasia, and Grace, Noah, Henigrace, Sophia, Mercy, Xander, Jessica and Zeke, who make life a stone groove!

Gratitude

Psalm 28:7 & Colossians 3:17.

Jim, often after I completed a piece you would read it, look bewildered, listen intently to my explanation, and then re-read with enlightenment and enthusiasm. Thank you for that and so much more!

Michelle Cavanaugh, thank you for not blocking my frequent "help me" texts and emails. You are wise and kind, Michi.

Mrs. Anne Rae, my grade one teacher who gently introduced me to letters and words and reading and writing and changed my life; Mr. Peter Fitzgerald, my junior high language arts teacher who sparked my interest in poetry and told me to never stop writing; and Professor Andrea Glover (Librarian Extraordinaire), whose creativity and passion for words reignited mine, thank you for being lights in my life.

Debra Campbell, Crowsnest Museum, Tammy Hansen, Jackie Hovan, Barbara King, John Kinnear, Rosalie Konynenbelt, Belle Kovach, Ethel Langhofer, Kim Miskulin, Kirsten Pries, Al Ritchie and Gary Ritchie, I am so grateful for your assistance with research, tracking down and/or providing photographs, offering feedback, and most importantly, for encouraging this common raven to fly.

> "Each of us is carving a stone, erecting a column,
> or cutting a piece of stained glass in the construction
> of something much bigger than ourselves."
>
> - Adrienne Clarkson

Table of Contents

Gratitude. v
Introduction xiii

Stone Foundation   1

Design Mined 2

Oldefar 3

Underpinning 4

The Strength of Stones 6

Agita 12

Carved In Stone 15

A Young Girl's Death 18

Stepping Stones. 19

Full Circle. 23

The Wayside Chapel. 26

Stone Stories: from A to Zed.   31

A. 33

Beaver Tale 36

Chalcedony and Charlotte Brontë's *Mementos* *38*

champs de patates 40

Dead of Night 42

Even 43

Facts: August 27, 1973 45

Found 46

Grindstone Island 48

Battleground 48

Crisscross 50

Friendly Fire 51

Hard to Understand 53

It's About Time 54

Jane Eyre: Chapter 35 56

Jump the Track 57

Just About Over 58

Kitjigattalik Stories 60

Living Stones 61

Completely About Mostly 61

Hereunder Unveiling Confoundedly
Penultimate Cabaret Choreography 62

Not on Your Life 66

Pass Words 68

Paucis Verbis 69

Sticks and Stones 70

Still and All 72

The Stone Rolled Away 74

Whinstones 75

Millstone 76

Mishmash 78

From *78*

Pastimes *79*

My Oh's 80

New Brunswick Rock Duck (Harlequin) *80*

Nine Words Wanting More *81*

November 82

Okanagan Drupe 83

Precious Stones 85

Qulliq 89

Rondeau quatre fois 90

Good Evening *90*

Nascent *91*

Pyrite *92*

Stone by Stone *93*

Seasonal Stone 95

(Version One) *95*

Seasonal Stone 96

(Version Two) *96*

Stoned 99

Stonewalled 102

Clipped Wings *102*

How Important is Known? *104*

writer's sleepwalk around block *106*

Truth Will Tell 107

Turquoise: Birthstone in Four Settings..........................108
  Carters Beach..*108*
  Keele River..*109*
  Little Limestone Lake......................................*110*
  Peyto Lake...*111*

Unerasing Places...112

Venus Gate, Rocktoberfest 2011.................................113

Winterstone..114

Xeriscaping..115

Yore: Áísínai'pi...116

Yukon Lazulite...117

Zed..119

End Notes **124**
Photograph List **125**
Reading List **128**
In Memory **135**

Introduction

Having spent my formative years in the Crowsnest Pass, my roots are embedded in stories of tragedy and triumph, both historically and personally.

For much of my life anxiety has been an eraser, erasing abilities, gifts, creativity and achievements, leaving empty spaces that too often filled up with doubt, defeat and depression. So although my passion for words is lifelong, the anxiety messages looping in my mind built seemingly impenetrable walls, blocking me from composing the book waiting within. Finally in January 2016, I committed a year to writing pieces and claiming my literary voice. With no plan, no direction and no theme, I just let the words lead. On a daily basis I prayed and worked under, over, around and with my anxiety. One year became two as I played with letters and words and patterns, and as the stone theme emerged, pieces about dancing and death, happiness and sorrow, faith and frailty, and people and nature fell into place. Like Stonewall, I had the time of my life as I discovered that "...there is no time like the present to make the most of time."

Thank you for picking up my book. I am curious, as you peruse my pieces, if you savour or shun, laud or despise, smile empathetically or frown emphatically "...will that change my workaday words?"

Design Mined

Just a stone's throw behind,

you will

find

you are

aligned,

combined,

intertwined

with,

defined,

inclined,

refined

by,

tribes and times

lang syned.

As stones study stones

Oldefar

Stone notes: One nest nets tons!

Underpinning

Quondam stones comprise my bedrock,
rugged roots not ordinary,
with pieces prior interlocked,
by a boundless lapidary.

Excavated from Aberdeen,
quandam stones comprise my bedrock,
cut, chiselled, cemented between,
patrimonial building blocks.

Stonemason Scots left from a dock,
sailed bravely to Ontario,
quandam stones comprise my bedrock,
quarried Ritchie stone mementos.

My granddad was a rolling stone,
travelled east to west, then took stock,
settled in a stone-shadowed home,
quandam stones comprise my bedrock.

As stones study stones

The Strength of Stones

Some grandmothers,
instead of quilted in smiling softness,
are chiselled out of stoic stone.

August 1919. Standing on a Liverpool pier, peering back at her life: career woman, buyer for a tony store, wanting nothing more than to be a lifelong London lady until chance and glance and dance and romance changed her circumstances and now she's a bride fighting her own war inside. Uncertainty and salt water streams wash over her and mingle with the dark choppy water lashing the sides of HMT Baltic, while next to her, facing forward, stands her Canadian Over-Seas Expeditionary Force fellow, glowing, knowing he's returning to the life he left behind. Unsure if love really will conquer all, she rubs her stomach, takes his hand, takes a ship, takes a train, takes a step forward in time, leaving her life behind as they journey to Bellevue.

September 1919. Standing at the Riverbottom train station. He looks up, sees his much-missed majestic mountain views, looks down at pebbly pathways, grins widely at familiarity and envisions possibilities everywhere. She looks down, sees her dusty, tired shoes, looks up at the forbidding grey monoliths, weeps at the starkness of the newness and foresees impassible obstacles everywhere.

But she's there, so she tries, days comprised of a stiff upper lip, ex-pat companionship, church teas and hymns, supporting him, washing babies and floors, all while trying to ignore her half-hearted heart. For completely accepting a new start isn't possible when it's impossible to get past the inescapable contrast between Dairy Road and Marylebone, and she frequently lies awake, questioning if it's all a mistake, aching for her beloved city.

So, a few years in she takes a chance, takes a train, takes a ship, takes a step backwards in time, leaves his life behind, trying to find her future in her past, but it doesn't last as her family summarily sends her back to Dairy Road. Knowing now she's there to stay, she walks determinedly through his doorway and she begins anew.

Truly, she gives her all to be a keen wife, keen mum, keen friend, keen member of the community, easing uncertainty through conviction and good deeds. She begins hosting Sunday roast dinners with puddings, puts out liquorice allsorts for all sorts, imports teas and treats, loyally keeps apprised of royalty, mourns King George like he's family, happily toasts Elizabeth in '53, and between newspapers, radio and then TV, stays ever-tuned to her Queen and country.

Thus, the years tarry yet hurry as they're apt to do and they work through untold challenges, manage family and finances, find themselves to be comfortable companions marvelling at their fortitude; but suddenly in '62 he leaves her in widow's weeds and she grieves, places flowers on his grave, then gravely stands alone in a space she's never fully embraced as her own.

For in spite of half a century on Dairy Road, it can never quite be home when melancholic roots lie parched under foreign soil; but she has a firm foundation and carries on bravely, a London lady right to the end.

After her service in '69, amid the teary smiles, the final goodbyes, her friends and family, her daughter and sons, their progeny both grown and young and the grandson who cherished her like a mum, lamented and sighed and wondered why she often seemed so blue. Perhaps if they had viewed her inward glooms, the constant repressing of her unrest, the stalwart suppressing of homesickness, how she often felt alone and adrift, they would have understood why they could never lift the veil of inherent sadness, that had shrouded her since she first peered back as she stood on a Liverpool pier.

Agita

Backdrop: 1960s.

There's some debate if Lake Natron actually turns animals into stone but I know a turtle can turn a town to stone;

I see the evidence every single day and I'm petrified.

Limestone forget-me-nots never let me forget that at 4:10 a.m. I could be sleeping and dreaming sweet dreams about doughnuts at Timmerman's bakery and be completely crushed and buried.

Please Don't Move Turtle

I plead
every   single   night;

Now I lay me down to sleep I beg the Lord to please keep

a

      rock

          avalanche

              off

                  of

                      me.

                        Amen.

As stones study stones

Epitaph:

Here lies THOMAS HUDDLESTONE.
Reader, don't smile!
But reflect as this tombstone you view,
That death, who kill'd him, in a very short while
Will huddle a stone upon you.[1]

Carved in Stone

Dairy Road.

Young sleepy summer day to fill, behind the dugouts faint rock-brushed trails lead up a hill and over, beckoning to the oft-forgotten Bellevue Union Cemetery, shrouded in solitude, thirsty wildflowers, mystery. Brittle grass beneath my feet postulates wariness but curiosity jumps over fences, eager to join a meandering unseen procession that's been drifting through the shadows since 1918.

Larch Avenue.

Old leaden wintered gate, careworn, taciturn, rattled by eager youthfulness, rustily creaks concern but I push through. Studying timeless texts my unmarked heart fissures, disturbed to learn that departures are not limited to those long in experience, that parts are sometimes brief. Much moved, inspired, I carve a dirge and a juvenile angst-filled foretelling eulogy emerges.

Camel's Hump.

Ageless yawnings spring forth a grave accent, ridge walking preceded by bitter gales singing strident tunes. Atop a rock cathedral I ponder, wondering if viewed monuments truly are dead ends or simply pauses, awaiting future authors' shrewd penned perceptions, imaginations. Time and floods and unkempt shrubs accrue but must not eradicate sources, words need faithful looking or they perish, erasing crucial pages from never-ending tomes.

A Young Girl's Death

She would not last long,
About to breathe her last breath,
About to face
A cruel, black death.

She thought of childhood days,
And the fun it was to play,
But the fun was only in thoughts,
And the thoughts were going away.

She smiled as she thought of her first dance,
Oh, how lovely it had been,
But then the loveliness became black,
And she let out a small, faint scream.

She thought of the children she'd never have,
And the unhappiness she now fought,
She thought of beautiful things,
Then suddenly, no longer she thought.

- M.D.McEachern School Poetry Submission (1972)

Stepping Stones

My precious piece of real estate
    with majestic mountain views
        where deer wander through
            and birds sing achingly sweet songs
                to friends and family long gone.

                                          Tuesday.
Dancing at a 1977 version of a sock hop, a precursor to Friday's prom; in slow motion my math teacher glides across the gym holding out his hand like he's asking me to dance but instead gestures me to follow. We're like Moses parting the Red Sea as dancers step aside to let us pass and I'm delivered through a door to a neighbour who whispers "your sister" while "Don't Leave Me This Way" echoes in the background.

Wednesday.

In line at Fantin's Funeral Chapel; told to go, that she's a beautiful little doll but she's a stone angel and I'm angry someone has slicked back her hair because she could do a Farrah better than anyone. And she's much too quiet now, this volatile 13-year-old child who once equally grumbled and giggled with abandon, and now well-meaning people murmur about how she looks so peaceful and I just want to shriek as I mutely shatter into a thousand buried pieces.

Thursday.

A school bus full of children on a field trip like no other, devastated and fascinated and maybe just a bit excited to get out of class to stand by a graveside. I also stand. Good stone soldiers obey orders and silently swallow grief and don't disturb the peace by weeping or laying down roses or screaming at the top of their voices as one by one everyone turns and leaves her all alone at Passburg Union Cemetery.

Friday.

The grad dress I picked out months ago is blue.

Monday.

Wisdom teeth extraction so impacted that I'm black and bruised with cheeks so puffed up they look like they are stuffed with the popcorn she once had waiting for me as a surprise when I got home from my job at the dairy.

Monday, next.

Back to school. The rumour is I had been absent because I was pregnant and all the pent-up anger that had no voice goes on a rampage and initiates an investigation news journalists would envy, tracing the tall tale to its creators and my first-ever published piece is a letter to the editor about Big-Mouthed Busybodies.

Life.
Going back is not permitted so I move forward. I know she isn't really there but still I care, so on April 12, 2006, I wrote a cheque so that he and me will someday reside at plots 33 and 34, row 12. Now on a day while others dance, I will lie beside her and on a headstone or bench plaque or just in the leaves of a tree planted in my memory, there will be a line to be read throughout time: Karen's Sister.

Full Circle

I close my eyes,
hitchhike to awakening,
turn the corner,
arrive at Jacques' merrymaking,
wearing moccasins
tucked beneath stonewashed bellbottoms,
inset with multi-flowerpower cotton.

The persistent winds of time waft by,
dispensing incense so intense
nostalgia amplifies,
scented by the essence of
drive-in burgers seared on both sides,
steaming hot dogs smothered in onions caramelized,
deep-fried crispy French fries.

Patricia Poriz

Rhinestone-studded ponies
draw me like a lodestone,
I sit astride, joyride,
serenaded
by pipe-organ overtones;
I'm Jane,
on my own private merry-go-round,
soaring high,
up and down,
up and down.

Grabbing the brass ring
a blue-ribbon tableau materializes,
and a wellspring of memories
lope past my eyes;
it's so inspiring,
latent buoyancy rises,
vibrantly colouring visualizing.

Sightseeing, I whirl contentedly,
downbeat's descending,
upbeat's ascending,
and ennui's set free;
hair whipping in the breeze,
I'm so pleased
that once again I've found,
biding bridled in the background,
the million-dollar view
that spurs my renewed
esprit to sing,
"Quelle belle vue!"

Patricia Poriz

The Wayside Chapel

As stones study stones

✝

For
many Sunday
afternoons, many
Sundays ago, after singing "Rock
of Ages" or "This Little Light of Mine"
or "Dreams of the Everyday Housewife" in
Mrs. Price's choir, I'd hike or bike to the little church,
when it was closer to Passburg. Little pews, little books, Mrs. Rae, animal
crackers, an alphabet above the blackboard: rays of light transforming
letters into worlds where it didn't matter that I was awkward and a little
bit odd and talked a lot about nothing hoping someone would understand
because I didn't. Sitting in a little church, in a little pew, reading little story
books, eventually browsing through the guest book, imagining the faces
and stories behind the signatures. I'd add a name or two, but not Patsy. Not
since page 20 in *My Little Blue Story Book* when Betty held out her doll
in the blue dress and said, "Mother! Mother! Here is Patsy. Come and see
Patsy!" and classmates laughed uproariously. So, instead I practiced cursive
and wrote Little Orphan Annie, New York City, and Ben, Polly, Joel, Davie
and Phronsie, Little Brown House, and Rich Little, Hollywood, California.
Did the keepers of the little church chuckle over the silly signatures or shake
their little heads and complain about disrespectful little sinners?

Not so many Sundays ago I lay in my prairie city bed, a little sleep, a little slumber, a 23-foot horse navigates into the bottomless blue of my eyes and I sail off through the night sky, following the illumination of a Burhinidae's yellow headlights. In the bow, Toni pitches out hailstones like baseballs, carving low reliefs onto unmarked limestone graves. Behind in the stern, Lucy grudgingly forgives the forsaking of my birth name, as we descend to the little church, now anchored in Bellevue.

When cravings coax a midnight repast late Jimmy appears, presenting a dinner for three seasoned with kalpasi, and I pay using stolen quarters from the bottom drawer of an earlier time. Sated we sit silently, reflectively. Moonkissed mercy breezes in, sorting through noble stones, tossing a white stone just out of grasp that floats past to Connelly, skipping playfully across the surface, sinking, hiding deep among the weeds so I can't read the name. Wading in I slip, stumble on an encrusted stone, poison permeates my soul, I heave, expelling long-held gastroliths that crumble at my feet, scraping the dead spots on my leaves, and pressured by the little lithops waiting in me, finite knowledge sifts through truth as stones study stones.

For many Sundays presently, prose from my sharpened stone remains obscure. Waiting for rays of light to transform letters into worlds, I sit contemplatively in a little church, in a little pew, reading *My Little Blue Story Book*.

Stone Stories: from A to Zed.

A

Funk; grey
granite island, isolated,
once a haven
for 200,000 Great
Auk, where they
could play
out of harm's way,
lay
singular eggs, stay.
In the 16th century that changed,
as sailors
came,
and instigated
a reign
of terror against
flightless penguins unable
to escape.
They
were chased,
mutilated,
separated
into pieces - meat, oil, fish bait -
or herded into boats - crated -
to accommodate
those awaiting
their downy feather freight.
The decimation
continued unabated
and by 1800, the Great
Auks were completely eliminated
from their rock of refuge. Heartbreaking.

Another baneful
story explains
how moral failure
ended in annihilation:
In 1840, the last remaining
British Isles' Great
Auk was taken
from its Stac-an-Armin birthplace,
conveyed
by three men to a ship, stowed away,
then four days
in blamed
for a raging
storm, superstitiously named
a witch and fatally
beaten; just an innocent babe
stoned to death, slain.
Disgraceful.

Now in case
you hope there may
be an enclave
of these original penguins someplace,
it's time to trace
the footsteps of the forsaken,
a shameful
abuse of power ending in total eradication.

In 1844, to satisfy the cravings
of a collector, three mates
sailed to Eldey Island and came
face-to-face
with Earth's last two auks bravely
guarding a priceless egg. The traders
debated
how best to enslave

their afraid
prey,
then strangulated
the dazed
Alcidae, erasing
our future nest egg. Paid
with pieces of silver, they
never calculated
the bitter aftertaste
of their betrayal.
Devastating.

Dear human race,
take this doomsday tale
about grave
mistakes
that erased
an irreplaceable
teammate
and advocate
for nature's
nonpareils whose fate
waits
upon agents
to give them space,
and keep them safe,
or someday
only frames
will be displayed
to portray
their greatness.
Don't delay
until it's too late!

Beaver Tale

Out you come, wrapped in soft luxurious potential, graced with finespun fins, free to swim and thus begin an odyssey that's new to you yet written in the depths of old. Observing, learning, blissfully crafting mud pies, devising ways to pick up sticks, engineering playhouses close to shore, you're simply innocence immersed in contentment.

Your course transforms when you display notable giftings, drumming scales on the surface so joyfully earnest, an impressed scout sends you out on stages far beyond the chambers of your isolated lodge. Venturing through uncharted channels early phrases appear melodic, trusting conductors like they're family but in truth you're just a commodity, hewn to feed predators disguised as allies.

Travelling the terrain you lumber along muddy roads, dragging notes through tattered trails, carrying chords for rootless rewards, thirsting to make a splash. And you're so hungry, once content snacking on aspen bark but your watermark keeps rising, consuming banquets with such abandon it leaves your table bare and you care less and less.

Yet more and more your habitat keeps expanding, everyone demanding another branch, your store is never full, so you keep slogging, logging, clearing paths until your structure is so vast it surpasses Wood Buffalo Park.

As stones study stones

Ultimately placed high upon an earthy throne, twigs spun into a gold-and-ammolite-covered robe, with streams of millions passing below, you finally bask in the trappings of idols.

Then inexplicably the tune changes, you're no longer the favourite, and fame is ebbing, dipping, sinking like a stone. Soon after your fur frays, and the praising fades, and you're drowning in a sea of negativity. For unfortunately, pond royalty is easily displaced, and upbeat is soon replaced by mudslinging tales splattered upon ragweed; and you're left watching incredulously as once adoring colonies drift away, aspiring for bigger-toothed stars on which to hook their claws.

But perhaps, Kit, it's not really a disaster but a new chapter, for just as pedestals are destined to topple over, departures offer new starts, so break-away. Chop down those empty mansions, sink unfulfilling distractions, trade in your eighteen carat sunglasses for the shade beneath the breezes of a cottonwood tree; construct a runway to calmer waters, float gently into illumination, release love songs from the heart, and swim free.

Chalcedony and Charlotte Brontë's *Mementos*

I'm not sure if you have heard about how
Aage Sorensen emigrated to Tryon, PEI, in 1928.

There's nothing strange
or unusual about that, in fact this
brings to mind my grandfather Alfred Jensen

who left Denmark with a mass
of emigrants in 1893. Alfred ended up settling in the

Prairies and of
course missed Denmark's blue waters, especially

while battling dust and droughts. But that's my ancient
history. Aage's story is the one I'm sharing,

and it's about treasures
or to be more specific, about how mementos
are stashed away even when they seem to be of

little value, kept to remind one of a past
event or just saved because they are a curiosity.

Now it pains
me to admit this but it's important to be upfront and
candid, so here it goes. Even though

one of my greatest pleasures
is writing anecdotes based on first-hand experiences, these
words are completely compiled from perusing volumes

As stones study stones

of articles about Aage. Anyway, in 1938,

while digging up potatoes, Aage clasped
onto what he thought was an arrowhead,

took it home, put it in a shaving kit along with
his toiletries, where it remained until his passing.

Fortunately that wasn't a costly
mistake, for in 1984, Aage's son Jack began asking

questions about that whatnot, and stone
the crows, what Jack discovered with
the assistance of others is worthy of being in print
evermore. For what Aage unearthed in that

red-soil potato patch wasn't simply an arrowhead at all
but rather an archive with an astonishing history

that has not faded
after nearly 11,000 years. Possibly PEI's

oldest manmade artifact, I'm not gilding
this wrap-up by saying Sorensen's Spearpoint

has its own story to tell about emigrants long gone.

champs de patates

Walk through the field,
Hear the stones murmur,
It's all just a puzzle,
Search for the whimsies.

Hear the stones murmur,
In devotional reverence,
Search for the whimsies,
In acres of pieces.

In devotional reverence,
A legend was planted,
In acres of pieces,
In the shade of Mont-Rigaud.

As stones study stones

A legend was planted,
It grew in a farmer's plot,
In the shade of Mont-Rigaud,
When he should have been resting.

It grew in a farmer's plot,
So he harvested the crop,
When he should have been resting,
On a Sunday afternoon.

So he harvested the crop:
Potatoes morphed into rocks!
On a Sunday afternoon,
Mull over this picture.

Potatoes morphed into rocks?
It's all just a puzzle!
Mull over this picture,
Walk through the field.

Dead of Night

A lumpy mattress stuffed with ill-equipped vulnerability,
underneath a bedspread dusted in potato-chip evasion,
supports her insecurities,
deferring unwelcome nocturnal beleaguering.

Her barricade,
bricked in by failsafe books,
stands on guard,
a soothing shield barring gloom's appearance,
until enervated eyelids begin to shutter,
allowing disquietude's darkest hours to seep in.

Unbidden,
disturbing, menacing fingers flare overhead,
spotlighting her shellacked-shut puzzle window,
igniting another ambush of dreary dread,
while she lies unsettled in a mouse-bed of unrest.

Discomfited by moans she's not prepared to probe,
vexed by groans that tiptoe stealthily
amongst the breaches in her shell,
she bolts,
aiming for a doorless door.

Searching blindly for a curtained getaway,
transporting ponderous secrets she doesn't even know,
she clambers up a steep ladder-rung stairway,
leaving in her wake,
chalkstone defences crushed to pieces.

Even

Smooth glossy flattish stones,

signed by guests then

placed unevenly in

my diaphanous vase,

keep me on an

even keel. Can't even

hope to articulate

what perusing

pebbly messages does

to my psyche. Even

during lonely,

dark days,

unmarked stones banked

beside an awaiting

blue marker cheers

me; trusting sometime soon

love will be penned

on my polished oddments.

Facts: August 27, 1973[2]

```
  S
G A W E L
  S
  K
F A R M
  T
  C A N A D A' S
  H
H E A V I E S T
  W             D
H A I L S T O N E
  N             S   T   C
                C L O S E
                E       D
                N       O
                D       U
          S O M E       X
          M     D     M
          A           R
    H A I L S T O N E S.
          L           S
  K I L L E D         K
          R           O
                      R
                      U
                      P
                      A'
                G E E S E
```

Found[3]

October 1, 1983.
James G. Wilson
and
Cecil Johnston
arrived at Castalia Marsh
to do some birding.
A bird
appeared
in
the
binoculars:
A songbird,
a most remarkable one,
that
perched on top of a dead
   alder.
It displayed
a
                   dark brown
                      crown,
the nape was a lighter
                      brown,
the breast and underparts were a
uniform tawny
                      brown,
the back and wings
were
                medium brown,
and
the bird
constantly flicked its tail
       vigorously up and down.

This mysterious visitor,
it was not a bird
they
had seen before,
and
the interesting question
about
            this occurrence
is how
        this species,
        this bird,
           a first autumn female,
arrived at the Bay of Fundy.
It
may have
darted out
from the east, by way of
      western Europe and the
      North Atlantic,
or
perhaps,
it took to the air
from the west via the
      Bering Strait, and on
      across North America.
However
this
maura or stejnegeri
came,
for
several minutes,
for several moments,

it flew past,
it flew
closer,
and
then
    flew off.
Thereafter,
two
more days
of
searching
proceeded,
but
the
rare
Siberian
could
not
be
located.
Nervous and agitated,
with
no
bird in hand,
an
out of sight,
out

of
    hope
black
light
might
have
flicked
on.
Fortunately,
painstaking scanning
and
focusing
during
that
first
morning
left
photographs
that
captured
the
Stonechat
as
it
sat
momentarily
on Grand Manan Island.

Grindstone Island

Battleground
(Église de Saint-Pierre-de-La Vernière)

Adrift in Saint-Pierre's burial ground,
looking uneasily around,
trying not to make a sound,
blending in the background,
hoping to stay unfound,
avoiding a lob's pound
that's on course in the playground,
where he's yanked, pushed, downed.

In the foreground,
framing a blue door watching spellbound,
driftwood messages from an earlier stound
creak and speak of other lives run aground,
shipwrecked pieces drowned,
found, blessed, milled, deemed sound,
nailed, pounded, crowned.

As stones study stones

These recovered walls, now renowned,
propone that he unbound,
and blast his truth about the unsound,
until an anchor is inbound.

So he bays like a basset hound,
beckoning for a fair ground,
where navigators sail in, dock, stay aground,
wait for his distress call, fall in, surround,
launch preservers that float upbound,
to ensure he's safe and sound,
shoring up his shiplapped rebound,
battening down his profound turnaround.

Crisscross

Great Blue Heron flies into tomorrow,
gliding over a Shepody Bay aviary,
thanks to a royal gift from long ago.

Casting a white-crowned shadow
atop a sheltered wetland sanctuary,
Great Blue Heron flies into tomorrow.

Rounded wings, graceful and slow,
descend, joining a flourishing colony,
thanks to a royal gift from long ago.

When to St. Anne an island he did bestow,
unknowingly King George the Fourth did guarantee,
Great Blue Heron flies into tomorrow.

Now majestic birds glide to and fro
because faith ministered with ecology,
thanks to a royal gift from long ago.

Past, present, future hovering may show,
random rulings are ordained in actuality;
Great Blue Heron flies into tomorrow,
thanks to a royal gift from long ago.

Friendly Fire

In the summer of nineteen sixty-five,
on an Ontario island retreat,
philosophies and principles arrive,
to enlist in an avant-garde sortie,
where passive defendants aim to survive,
by employing an irenic entreat,
against a tyrannical invasion,
galvanized by a right-wing persuasion.

For thirty-one hours, thirty-one factors,
mistrust, miscommunicate, misdirect,
resulting in chaotic reactors,
broken by their conviction disconnect,
allowing non-violence detractors,
the ability to conquer unchecked;
leaving Grindstone's Experiment in shreds,
and lessons scattered amongst thirteen dead.

Hard to Understand

You ask mountains but we build hills,
scarred hands tilling earth
over mounds of ice, misconstrued
sacrifices eroded black
by scorching winds,
roused by misread codes.
Lost sheep bleat weakly
yet still are heard, but our
whispered words just disappear,
reappearing as misquotes in future
trials, wielded as spears drawing
thick blood from drained
hearts, splattering barren
fields. Turmoil sowed
grows futile vines
leaving thirsting scions
choking down rusty wine
poured through cracked
faltering lips,
pleading pure but endlessly
discerned as unclear.
Effort slumps when doublespeak
converts well-intentioned deeds
to sullied soil, piled against
feet pierced by vacillating quills
armed with toxic barbs. Defeated we retreat,
hurled headlong over stumbling stones,
our vanquished hopewell bones
settle despondently upon craggy paths,
curved by divergent fault lines.

It's About Time

Sometimes, one believes there's no time to lose,
puts on running shoes, hotfoots through time.
Other times, the race against time
leaves one gasping for breath,
hunched over regrets,
hobbling timorously down the home stretch.
Oftentimes, it's a marathon,
seems unceasing, like a bowhead
wearily facing hurdle after hurdle.
Every time, the course is short and time is swift,
passes by like a mayfly,
barely spreads its wings,
flaps a fleeting dash,
and in next to no time,
the sands of time have flitted by.
From time immemorial, the time between
birthtime and burytime,
be it long distance or a sprint,
cross country or a trail run,
aerobic or anaerobic,
a world record or last place,

that space is your lifetime;
and no matter what the speed or pace,
the cheers or jeers that one has faced,
for all there is a time and place
where time will tell and then compel
the stopwatch to call time.

As stones study stones

Once upon a time there was a man nicknamed Stonewall, and for him it was a time to build. He didn't take the time to disclose the purposes of his heart, even when skeptics would tell him he was wasting time. Stonewall could have passed his time having an easy time, spending time in common pursuits, and from time to time he would try to do as others; but time and again, he would mourn it as lost time, and at that point in time he would get back on track. Any time Stonewall was asked how much more time before he would taper off, he'd stretch his timeworn muscles and reply "Sometime." Now there were times Stonewall had a heck of a time, like the time part of the stone structure collapsed and he had to work overtime to get it rebuilt. What a time he had! As years ran into decades, many a time spectators would coach, tell him he was on borrowed time, that it was time to slow down, but each time he would shrug and say there is no time like the present to make the most of time. Long slow distance, that was Stonewall's timeless philosophy; for what's thirty years of gathering, positioning, balancing thousands times thousands times thousands of stones, all on your own, if you're having the time of your life! It was just a matter of time, hour by hour, day by day, until determination became actualization, and Stonewall certainly earned his time to laugh as he wrote "The End" on the final stone of the Great Wall of Saskatchewan. Let's be clear, Stonewall didn't know his appointed time, or if he would be granted the time to see his vision to completion so that he could be deemed a legend in his own time. Yet, as if he had all the time in the world, Stonewall took it one step at a time, trusting that dedication to his personal best would stand the test of time. And honestly, during question time, what will matter least to the timekeeper: did not start or did not finish?

Jane Eyre: Chapter 35[4]

"between the stones and fallen rafters,"

Existence desolate wandered alone racing despair.

Every direction walked a recalled desert,

"dead as the stones."

Eyes dark with aged ruins determined

"he would not cross the door-stones of the house."

"between two stone pillars crowned by stone balls,"

Judicious absent nobly entered.

Jaded answers now explained

"the grim blackness of the stones."

Jewel accepted novel engagement,

"sharing the shelter of his narrow marble house."

Jump the Track

Hop to it
Hop skip and jump
Jump the fray
Jump in feet first
First in line
First and last
Last but not least
Last out
Out of breath
Out of step
Step on the gas
Step right up
Up to the challenge
Up and running
Running around
Running well
Well and good
Well dressed
Dressed to the nines
Dressed to kill
Kill the clock
Kill two birds with one stone
Stone cold
Stone dead

Dead end
Dead draw
Draw line
Draw fire
Fire in the hole
Fire back
Back to the drawing board
Back in the game
Game plan
Game that two can play
Play to win
Play hard to get
Get walking papers
Get somewhere fast
Fast lane
Fast speed
Speed away
Speed by
By the sweat of your brow
By moving on
On the right foot
On the right track
Track time
Track record
Record...
Time...

Just About Over

Over and over and over,

flying over, hovering over,
looking over gravel-edged shallowness,
enduring layovers, endless sleepovers,
in a quest to uncover a safe stopover.

Overcast skies hang

over and over and over,

until overtired feather-light cryptic pullovers
pass over a desolate hope and opt to stay over,
and overjoyed

tangerine
leggings
dance,

marking their undercover canvas.

As stones study stones

Brooding overflows until overarching oblivion?
overt disregard?
overlooks bedcovers and takes over,

and overstepping movers and Rovers
run over,
roll over,
make over,
a camouflaged refuge,
into a dump of leftover spillovers,

where predators peruse and nature loses,
and overthrown plovers mourn

                              over and over and over,

piping plaintive peeps overhead,

as overwrought winds
erase all the traces
of innocently sweet,

                              inward
                         turned
                            feet,

on sand overruled by gravel-edged shallowness.

Kitjigattalik Stories

These deposited manuscripts are not plotted
where scripts run through centuries, outlining

who   how   why

decisions, expeditions;

nay, existence was not english,

black and white

ghostwritten

clichéd printed letters

addressed and dispersed for impending proofreading.

Instead, these chert diaries are signposts
where scribbles run through centuries, outlining

who   how   why
decisions, expeditions;
aye, existence was nuanced,
greyish, rusty and black,
first-person written
knapped
novel
tools,

trademarked and dispersed for impending proofreading.

Living Stones

<u>Completely About Mostly</u>
(Proverbs 26:17)

As a rule, people like
to hear their own voice, often one
eager word after another, about who
knows what. Many times, fear grabs
problems best left without a
continual nudging. On average, stray
conversation is overly critical. Commonly, a dog
benefits from praise; teaching by
goodness with constant presence, the
love invested connects. Mainly, human ears
become filled with delving bodies which is
rather trying. For the most part, someone
is sure to storm toward those who
would prefer neglect. Typically, awareness rushes
to intrusive attention, showering righteous raindrops into
overtaken backyards. Almost always, futile prying about a
completely private realm will likely initiate a public quarrel.
Usually sincere praying, not
stoning, carries healing flowers. Most often, their
life clashes need not be your own.

Hereunder Unveiling Confoundedly
Penultimate Cabaret Choreography

Chandelier visionary
decorate progression,

peyote stimulates
dandelion elephant
imaginings

awaiting
machinist
falsetto
feebleminded
airsickness
demeaning
augustness

glassblowing alarmingly
adamant
buffalo tumbleweed
absolutes

following
        billowing
                wallowing
                        shallowness

exhuming jitterbugging
sinister
stubbornness

As stones study stones

Scorekeeping
detestable highwayman

navigate
volcanic
barbequed
pilgrimage
rebuttals

prolonging
rainforest
cyanide
belittling
hiccupping

Bulletproof
chimera

muddleheaded
depository

quarantine
frivolous grenadine stepsisters

lobbying
decadent
refreshments
postseason

Standoffish
nefarious
allegory

elaborate aversion

thereupon unsettling
metaphors surrounding
taskmistress distrustful

drearily
sidestepping
examining damnatory
liable
unsweetened
slipstreaming

Headwaiter
onlooker

foreseeing
insipid
disgraceful

withdrawing
unlovely
distrustful

Eloquent carpenter

jimmying
disheartened
distillers'
homily

overhearing
glamorous
sightseeing
vagabond
daydreamers

acclaiming
fricasseed
everlasting
blackmailers

Henceforward
decorate progression,

pithily
examine
winnowing
caramel cobblestone
untoward
unhopefuls
shimmying

enjoying
unenlightened
confounding
magazines

inhaling chocolate

hobbyhorse
contumelies.

Not on Your Life

beside the see,
shadow others play,
compelled by slate-stamped plots
to plant the nots under ashen skies.

we believe, becoming silhouettes,
snared by a hedge of thorns and thistles,
where creeping lips whisper,
you're not worth a damn,

and as vulnerable inner mechanisms
trigger boundless whys,
passing personalities cultivate dolls' eyes,
twining shallow roots around
a stoneheap of malevolence:

   not noticed
  not seen, not heard
 not enough: not now, not ever
 not bright, not capable, not valuable
not respected, not desired, not important

loved?

absolutely not! not a hope in hell.
not in my book. not on my watch.

As stones study stones

Beside the see,
veiled passion plays,
compelled by gem-stamped thoughts
to plant the nots under mustard skies.

We believe, becoming whole,
sheltered by a circle of cypress and myrtle,
where verdant lips whisper,
do not be afraid.

And as vulnerable inner mechanisms
trigger boundless praise,
graceful gardeners cultivate scarlet blaze,
wrapping deep roots around
a bedrock of benevolence:

Not alone
Not invisible, Not voiceless
Not inadequate: Not now, Not ever
Not foolish, Not useless, Not worthless
Not despised, Not unwanted, Not insignificant

Loved?

Doubt not! Hope will not be incinerated.
Not in My book. Not on My watch.

Pass Words

Look up! Do eyes hear, say what the ear drums?

At night, stand with power, fully on guard, rail in hand, made for vision.

Less care is over; analyze food, stuff below door, way under. Take rod of gold, fish dark out, look new, born over, coming in, capable, sound.

Proof: read to end, play of life; time piece, work finger, print letter, head into city, wide streets make.

Shift to field, trip over fire, place ash in ear, mark as news, cast out. Back further, more takes place.

Kickers called dead lock in, fuse back, pack hay, ride horse; power may fly in, bred upon water, logged as love.

Sick of common? Place change over rain, coat brain, wash, stand under arch.

Angels of stone, walled in brick, work here after dark. Some fly, blown by joy, ride over earth, quake sea, worthy to give.

Away you run, around life, boats low, land in mud, slide over moon, struck by lamp, post text, book seat, belt side, light heart, burn doubt, fully cross road, house throne.

Will your ear ring? Let down follow up,
holding merry, making eye salve.

Paucis Verbis

What would Jesus do?

Do I presume to know

His thoughts,

His ways,

His whys,

except in part?

What did Jesus do?

How quickly I forget

His love,

His grace,

His passion,

the touchstones

for my part.

Sticks and Stones

As my friend I sought you out, not having a moment's doubt
that in my pain and grief, you'd be offering
kindness and charity, but what you called loving
was so notched with judging that I was caught off guard,
vexed you could be so hard, but perhaps you can't see
what my heart really needs, if your grace has been displaced
by the log jammed in your eye.

I accept exhortations tendered as warm suggestions
or earnest corrections, but your oration
sounds like condemnation, and I feel bowed and bruised
by your harsh attitude and negativity
regarding my hurting; so I'll state I'm concerned
what you think you discern, may actually be blurred
by trees rooted in your eye.

Next, you defend your beliefs about what you think I need
based on your scrutiny of the codes and creeds;
with proud ability you start to pick and choose
phrases to match your views, leaving me quite confused,
and even more bemused, about how you perceive
with any certainty, if your insights are blighted
by the stump wedged in your eye.

As stones study stones

Then honestly I suffer, when later I discover
that in front of others you audaciously
list my deficiencies, then issue a decree
for crucial prayer for me; I'm so sad and distressed,
but it's true I confess, it's taxing to foresee
how much I need mercy, if your view is being skewed
by timber lodged in your eye.

Oh, Miserable Comforter...

Now, paradoxically before you I stand and plead,
needing forgiveness please for my scorn unleashed,
my excessive chiselling that rots grace and peace.
Now may we move ahead and plan to leave unsaid
words scarce in heart content that knot up and torment,
and aim for love instead, so we can easily tread,
unencumbered by lumber.

Still and All
(1890s-1920s)

All days like grass flourish,
ploughing, sowing, reaping,
such are the paths for all,
wheat and weeds, all told;
still, the sun will step aside
and in the still of winter's night,
just beyond a stone gateway,
still strangers wait, all sharing space.

impartial: strove in a firm fashion to dispense mercy and compassion
and smiled softly at the future.
narrow-minded: views were unkind, short-sighted, blind, until in the
bitterness of death, wrath was past.
tight-fisted: amassed bread for self alone, in the final measure all that
was grown was figs from thistles.
enigma: whistled hope, cited light, divvied fruit, gifted mites; robe sewn
with blue, purple, and crimson.
reticent: hymns in quietness raised, worked humbly, counted days, hid
deeds, and gained a wise heart.
vainglorious: part trumpet, part practised piety, played a part much
envied, but it was waste and void.
aphotic: destroyed hope, trampled dreams, teemed with hostility, and
departed with no one's regret.
lily-white: set time heartbreakingly brief, but grief's mustard seed faith
believed, not lost but gone before.

As stones study stones

Passages pause like a sigh,
all different but still the same,
all lying still at Laurel Hill,
amid the shuffling of laden feet,
the remains of pokerfaced relief,
the lingering of poignant tears;
still within octagonal walls,
all wait for the earth to thaw.

The Stone Rolled Away

Art

cast

glint

amidst

haziest

abstract

blueprint.

Worthiest

Sunburst,

Holiest

Spirit,

Light

sent

art.

Whinstones

Wept waits, while wasted wayfarers, wheedled wittingly with wily weasel's war waltz, waive waiting wagons, woodenly wooing whiskey-weathered warship's wildcat wellspring.

Wept walks while wounded warriors wander, wild walleye wonderers watching walls wrinkled with waterlogged willpower, washing wince-worthy waysides with whistle-wet wailings.

Wept whets while wanton wildfires wane, wafting wombat-wisdom workers with windblown watchwords, waiting with wholehearted welcome when world-weary warthogs whisper weak worn why-words wanting worth.

Wept wades with woeful,
wiping weather-whipped windows,
whitewashing waterloos,
writing warranties without waivers,
watering wilted wildflowers
with warm wagered wine.

Millstone

Open the door of her
deep dusty pantry
and look. Middle shelf, at the back,
hidden, but it's still there,
in the shadows,
just past your reach:
key, thimble, sword, mallet, armadillo, list.

Sixteen.
Finally seen. Imprisoned but
now liberty: a
Folger Adam brass key
locking out the enemy.
No longer his
writhing unclothing nothing plaything.
Packed in boxes,
best forgotten,
it's still life.

Twenty-two.
Small breakthrough. Peter, short,
skinny, ill-at-ease, but she sees
peace so tentatively hands him a
tiny tin thimble game piece.
He accepts and begins quietly
kithing betrothing bequeathing everything,
to
their still life.

Twenty-six.
Quick fix. Secret afternoon
libation; olives speared with a
3.5" vintage Toledo cocktail sword
drowning in the accidental
birthing bathing teething girl-thing,
who's
disturbing still life.

Forty-two.
No clue. Unglued by
perplexing pressing offspring,
mouthing frothing loathing seething,
throwing a plastic green mallet
at ice block dripping in gin and leaving
impenetrable still life.

Sixty-seven.
Sudden procession. Always there,
accepting, interceding, until unexpected
passing burying wreathing grieving;
clutching his wooden bobble-headed Mexican armadillo,
she's retreating into a
stony still life.

Eighty-four.
Closed door. Decade old
list on stationery bordered with purple hyacinth
tucked away. Step 8 complete but
9 still waits. Should have, could have, words for
smoothing soothing something anything,
forever unsaid.
Her still life.

Mishmash

From

START
of a ridiculous post
to
the different ears:
Go near,
to
the dawn.
Cradle God's sublime word soup.
Go far,
to
the bottom,
to
the grave,
TO
your pillar,
to
your dusk. Heart nuts angle
the lips
to
get
the riches
to
the rags
and
FINISH.

Pastimes

...skipping Mr. Simon can jump the red checkers...

...Rover and Wolf kick cat's light green marbles...

...robbers crack cradle, hide Chinese red stones...

...cops whip rope, go "freeze!"...

...what???

       Mother says it is tag time and I may seek the light!

My Oh's...

New Brunswick Rock Duck (Harlequin)

Oh, that I
could be you, slate
blue, chestnut, white,
black-striped totem pole, for
you show that life is best lived
courageously. You lords with
your ladies, small in size,
may whistle mousey cries, but that just disguises your brave
hearts. You could circumvent the Wolf, chart a course steered
by fear, stay sheltered safely near undemanding, smooth-
sailing wet lands, tepidly withstanding life's winter seasons,
languishing in milk-and-water wastelands. No,
you risk broken bones, plunge
into turbulence, knowing
pluck won't grow unless
you fly into adversity.
So, you test your
capabilities, explore,
turn over stones, strive
more and more, instead of
clowning around cautiously offshore.

As stones study stones

Nine Words Wanting More

Oh,
to
own
a
silver
coin
with
drusy
stone.

November

For John Dan White & James Robert (Bob) Glover

> Commit to no stone left alone,
> place a poppy on a headstone,
> with a solemn, respectful tone,
> commit to no stone left alone.
> May we never forget to show,
> their sacrifices are well known;
> commit to no stone left alone,
> place a poppy on a headstone.

Okanagan Drupe

How passionately they reach for you,

my hankering bruising fingers;

caress blushing lusciousness,

expose fleshy sweetness,

drip juicy ripeness,

clinging to a

sensuous

summer

fling.

Precious Stones

Sardonyx

Multi-layered favoured one,
with iron-willed eloquence aptly carved into a unique cameo;
striped
stone of strength,
courage, happiness.

Garnet

Inspiring, deep pomegranate-red-hued gem of faith,
rest comfortably in vibrantly vitreous handsomeness;
strive
for peace, happiness, deep friendships.

Pearl

Graciously lovely preference,
greatly valued for
rare iridescent lustre, naturally created
with concentric internal layers,
drawn from exotic waters.
Captivatingly unique majestic masterpiece, strung elegantly
with
purity,
kindness, innocence.

Peridot

Brilliantly bright, exceptionally endeared, glimmering evening emerald,
remarkably gleaned from meteorites, earth's mantle, lava;
one-colour treasure presented in innumerable shadings,
imparting prosperity, peace,
and health-giving happiness to the
wise.

Amethyst

Wintertide; just after sunrise, just before sunset,
as sun's compassion
bathes cold, dark days in forgiving rays of wispy soft, warm
        gossamer light,
durably
ardent royal-purple luminosity ignites bracing dreams,
        steeped in courage, serenity, peace.

Emerald

Eminently esteemed emblem, emulating a wellspring of
        intensely verdigris lushness,
keep
defending the view that true flaws emote genuineness,
emphasizing
acceptance protects
crystal clear transparency, emanating patience, peace,
        tranquillity.

Tourmaline

Conceptualize creativity,
electrically
charged by sagacious minerals rainbow-riding, harnessing,
        interlacing,
releasing rich ranges of engaging colours; then behold
        fascinating,
out-of-earth compositions, wrangling
strength, peace and
calm.

Ruby

Exceptionally substantial crimson-cheeked king of
        preciousness, heart glowing with fiery vitality,
reign successfully
with noble energy, courage, confidence,
rectitude and strength.

She sets about her work vigorously;

her arms are strong for her tasks.

She sees that her trading is profitable,

and her lamp does not go out at night.

- Proverbs 31: 17-18

Qulliq

Carved

stone lamp,

survival

necessity,

light and heat her responsibility;

attentively watching, guarding, tending,

sustaining life.

Fitfully

sleeping;

long

night

winter

smouldering,

flaring, glowing,

illuminates the keeper of the flame.

Rondeau quatre fois

Good Evening

Theirs is the night; in the twilight,
furtively gliding, not by sight
seeking a stray larvae buffet,
drifting through a moonlit ballet,
undulant adagio delight.

Despite a venomous birthright,
hushed vesper mellowness takes flight;
eventide allongée soirée,
theirs is the night.

Hushed parting evensong invites
dawn, shy shifting shadows alight,
lie low, catnap, dream day away,
under Milk River stones they stay,
biding midsummer eve's backlight,
theirs is the night.

Nascent

Old age bitterness, to carefree
blossoming summer-kissed beauty,
is inconceivable; instead,
perennial, yellow tinged-red
crowned heads of youth believe, not me.

With shining star viridity,
rosette lance-leaved tufted glory,
they're just too succulent to dread,
old age bitterness.

The truth that youth will grow weary
is just myth and hyperbole,
to resilient stone-sown roots thread
with naivety; fading's ahead,
but sitting-fresh crops can't foresee,
old age bitterness.

Pyrite

All that glitters, catches the eye,
shimmers, may be but a false fly
cast on the water, a trap door
skillfully patterned in gold or
chic amber or tiger print ply.

For as churning stone nymphs drift by,
crafty match-the-hatch posers try
to ensure stoked rainbows explore,
all that glitters.

Pot of gold promises may lie,
dead drift, tumble, splatter, apply
alluring "come-hither for more
gold digger" lines and hooks, all for
the prize, a rise inveigled by
all that glitters.

Stone by Stone

You walk among stones, like Andrew J.,
and I want to explore, someday,
remote wilderness with alpine
meadows, rock faces, genuine
untouched thin places - your byway.

A skid-slip stone Muncho trailway,
stone-on-stones, stone pillars, and grey
Inukshuk guides all underline,
you walk among stones.

Your rock-ram-band go-your-own-way
creed calls my stone-drawn heart to pray
that you will graze, unscathed, by mines
and strips, on Todagin's cloud nine
cliffs, as horn riffs forever play,
you walk among stones.

Seasonal Stone

(Version One)

Peculiar pearly whites gnawingly mock me,
dull prisoner in unlit chambers, all exits blocked,
liberation by alliteration pending.

Lowland mitts tapping irked curved claws,
groggily brood over cloudless probability, manacle me impotent,
interned by influential climatologists.

Heavy corpse slogs cowering limbs loathly,
dark familiarity uproots sunlit risk, thaw force recedes,
prorogued by habitual disturbance.

Foggy kip wrestles unwelcome duty rouse,
great late bear radar nudges, yields ogling upwards,
ordained by turtle back.

Pelage frosted bachelor orb lethargically transforms,
innate prevails, bristly tail quickens, hope is awakened,
surged by dormant inclinations.

Deuce signal game whistle upward trudges,
small rise courage refulgent sputters, spring snub retreat,
shaded by shifting shadows.

Stern kindred Yukon Woodchuck worthy,
buoyant luminosity clearing then freezes, gloom emerges bitter,
pressured by sad inevitability.

Seasonal Stone

(Version Two)

Peculiar pearly whites gnawingly mock me,
dull prisoner in unlit chambers, all exits blocked,
liberation by alliteration pending.

*BTW DYK, as a political protest Punxsutawney Phil may be immigrating
to Canada? Becoming home to such a preeminent weather-predicting
woodchuck would be a stupendous coup. In anticipation, a committee has
been formed to fast-track resettlement. #movingtocanada*

Lowland mitts tapping irked curved claws,
groggily brood over cloudless probability, manacle me impotent,
interned by influential climatologists.

*IIRC, Brock Jellison danced up a storm with his talented tapping feet at the
2010 Winter Olympics.*

Heavy corpse slogs cowering limbs loathly,
dark familiarity uproots sunlit risk, thaw force recedes,
prorogued by habitual disturbance.

*DM. On January 27, 1962, there was a tremendous thaw in Pincher
Creek, compliments of a commoving Chinook, which raised the
temperature from -19C to +22C in one hour.*

Foggy kip wrestles unwelcome duty rouse,
great late bear radar nudges, yields ogling upwards,
ordained by turtle back.

*BIF, due to her high degree of determination at the 2008 Summer
Olympics, Carol Huynh was hailed as a hero when she became the first
Canadian citizen to earn a gold medal in women's wrestling.*

Pelage frosted bachelor orb lethargically transforms,
innate prevails, bristly tail quickens, hope is awakened,
surged by dormant inclinations.

*AFAIK, Sherbrooke, Québec, and Thunder Bay, Ontario, tie for the
shortest frost-free season in Canada.*

Deuce signal game whistle upward trudges,
small rise courage refulgent sputters, spring snub retreat,
shaded by shifting shadows.

*TBH, I was blown away when the top five responses to my survey seeking
suggestions for Canada's most esteemed whistleblowers were Kerry Fraser,
Jennifer Anavi Davies, Bill McCreary, Linda Parker Hamilton, and the
Friendly Giant. Oh, Canada, was this an aberrant anomaly, or a gauge of
cold-front oblivion?*

Stern kindred Yukon Woodchuck worthy,
buoyant luminosity clearing then freezes, gloom emerges bitter,
pressured by sad inevitability.

TSNF

Stoned

Just another apple auctioneer,
    chanting wiles high
above agony
    or imperfect or

                    hamster wheel ordinary,

    selling extraordinary relief
that you want to believe,
so you bid your fool's gold
and the hammer says sold
    and you buy and fly higher than the

                    London Eye ride.

Just another apple appetite,
    conjuring euphoria high
above anything, undermining everything,
to satisfy fruitless cravings.
    So you

                hide
            sigh   cry
            deny   ply
              lie

    leaving behind applesauce
promises to pacify
    hungering standbys.

Patricia Poriz

Just another apple aria,
   casting whys high
above dizzying dreams,
awash in somniferous streams,
    rippling from the skipping of soapstone and marble:

        build bridges   won't enable
   be a soft place to fall   be tough
       safe site   guarding my all
     you're welcome   stay away
     let's start anew   it's hopeless
      we're hopeful   that's it, we're through
       we love you   we hate you
           what should we do?

   And the more stones
that are thrown, the higher
   you go, chasing your ether paradise.

Just another apple addict,
   cursing consequences high
above the upset carts,
smashing life apart,
   leaving you

          impaired
      impoverished   imprisoned
        immured

As stones study stones

but you persevere,
bidding higher
and higher,
   chasing one more bite,

   until blight overtakes,
and the final score states,
poisoned fruit won
   and you're done.

Just another apple adieu,
   choking eulogies high
above another picked pome,
lying low in a cairn-covered abode,
   while mourners' agonies fly higher than the
                        High Roller ride,

wanting
imperfect you
   and wishing for

                  hamster wheel ordinary.

Stonewalled

Clipped Wings

I long to close the door on metrical logical versification and write
esoteric dark musings with jagged incomplete sentences and words so
brilliantly unclear that reading poets sanction perusal.

I inwardly, latently, long to thoroughly, completely, close
the tarnished dented door on orderly metrical mundane
logical lucid vanilla versification and, alternatively, write wise
epic esoteric deep dark mystical musings with wondrous jarring jagged
imperfectly incomplete sinuous sentences,
and, also, warble words so surprisingly, brilliantly, brazenly,
unbelievably unclear, that truly respected reading
plumed poets sanction serious, prompt perusal.

I inwardly, latently, long to, thoroughly, *when
White-breasted Nuthatch's yank yanks*, completely close
the tarnished dented door on orderly metrical.

Mundane *knocking knocking knocking knocking*
logical lucid *knocking knocking knocking knocking knocking*
vanilla versification *knocking knocking knocking knocking*
goes unanswered and *so I* alternatively write:

mimicking wise *Great Horned Owl's* epic esoteric *hoo hoo*
pinching Gray Catbird's deep dark *chek chek*
impersonating Red-breasted Sapsucker's waah waah mystical musings
tinkering with *Pileated Woodpecker's* wondrous *wuk wuk*
imitating Ruddy Turnstone's jarring jagged *chuckle chuckle*
simulating Black-capped Chickadee's imperfectly incomplete *dee dees*
murmuring Tufted Titmouse's sinuous *peter peter* sentences
and also *duplicating Dark-eyed Junco's kew kew.*

Warble words *hoo chek waah wuk chuckle dee peter kew*
are so surprisingly, brilliantly, brazenly, unbelievably unclear, that truly,
respected reading *doesn't deserve* plumed poets' sanction *of Blue Jay's jeer*
jeer jeering.

Serious prompt perusal: *Common Raven, I, may never fly across the*
Great Rift Valley. Will commending choruses ever call?

How Important Is Known?

If I become familiar or remain unseen, does that change my workaday words? Will my neologisms become wisdoms if celebrated?

My unconscious connected to my thumb wrapped around a Venus Velvet 6557 HB and cryptically announced,

pangs standing parched thirst for gushing talents.

If you under no circumstances scan that sentence, if it never enters through your lens and makes your brow furrow, causing your synapses to perform a jerky dance whereby you either get it and see an image or decide it's just a string of words not worthy of printing, do those words still matter?

Sometimes I am a passenger in a car where the driver prefers quiet even though my lips are quivering, so I glance broodingly out the window and P & H Milling Group hints to me that

standing alone full grinds few good grains for empty silos.

If before you peruse my musings it had been decided that my contemplations were notable, would you be more likely to mull it over, want to dig deeper, see my picture?

As stones study stones

Right left wrong standing over stagnant stones.

I can spend a week on a phrase because it refuses to be enlisted alongside second-class trite expressions, and when I finally convince it to affix, I'm victoriously due a medal. But a struggle always ensues between fighting for acknowledgement or retreating under my down comforter of obscurity; for if I should become significant, will my words turn against me? Will your interpretations smudge my pages, transforming shadowy imaginings into off-base assumptions?

Out was standing before in because question asked last first.

I do worry if I'm published and hand over my key, you will storm into my glass house built with sheets of metaphors and mystery and smash it into shards; and while a few wide-eyed wanderers might pick up my pieces and share them with strangers, I fear misreads will mutter malisons against me.

If

see sees because say says something,

where should I be standing?

writer's sleepwalk around block

dark hours passively mount wavering horses,
carried swiftly past owls wafting away,
above dusky observers murmuring obscure suspicion,
beyond dogmatic peddlers mocking metaphoric words.

see stanzas weaving stories between stars,
high rising tired riddles dissipating time;
flying diatribes plot, hindering elevation's visit,
keeping sceptical verses scorning resolution's score.

losing maxims commence vapid composing battle,
fighting rhetorical rival choruses directing change;
loose sarcastic tongues pack foe's cannon,
shooting captious throes, causing thoughtless pain.

piercing scruples rise, eclipsing silence's scream,
no dilemma solves without rolling dice;
toss customary hooks, superficial coax out,
in revisions engage keystones anchored deep.

dry authors crave turquoise drizzle run,
cry for practice, young ardent wolf;
vicious winds divulge hidden vision circle,
blue connects place to allegorical moon.

Truth Will Tell

He will
walk the Chimney Trail,
mindful that buried pasts haunt future lives,
and darkness must be exposed to light,
or it just seeps deeper and deeper.

She will
saunter past two stone chimneys,
bow her head respectfully,
then gaze up at the clouded stories,
subtly scribed on sky-blue stationary.

They will
wade into past wrongs and rights,
pause, contemplate, and scrutinize,
what remnants and relics symbolize,
through the lens of different views.

We will
not hide if we seek:
peek past beliefs based on pre-assembled pieces,
look for concepts conveyed as concrete releases,
find perceptions primed under coloured verses.

History can be twisted, that must be known,
or we become nothing more than Death Valley stones,
blindly rolling along, leaving tracks lacking veracity.

Turquoise: Birthstone in Four Settings

<u>Carters Beach</u>

Blue
lips aren't
amiss when
you've been tricked by
a teasing, turquoise
tropical illusion,
whitewashed with sparkling soft sand,
fanned across an exceptional
three-in-one beach wonderland. Still, a
wee chill is worth the thrill of dipping toes
to expose a hidden treasure trove of
sand dollars; or for the brave, diving
in to gaze at amazing sea
life. Really, it's no surprise
even evergreens stand
pleased, drinking in this
Nova Scotian
Atlantic
Ocean
belle.

Keele River

Iced turquoise

diced by ripples and riffles

spliced with swift rapids

sliced through by true-blue paddlers

enticed by white-water courage.

Little Limestone Lake

Out of limestone ground waters flow,
till bit by bit marl crystals grow,
and slowly sink and wait below,
to start the show, to start the show.

The cool marl lake seems incomplete,
so coaxing nature's turquoise feat,
impatient blue-winged teals entreat,
"turn up the heat, turn up the heat!"

Then summer sun comes out to play,
igniting a divine display:
a turquoise to egg-blue array,
that gilds the day, that gilds the day.

Peyto Lake

Peyto

lying in wait

for its glacial grindstone

magical rock-flour reflected

turquoise.

Unerasing Places

Stone's Cove, I

know your deep-rooted histories were unearthed,
efficiently converted to house boats,
hauled across troubled waters,
resettled elsewhere into new berths,
leaving behind rugged foundations
and pensive weathered markers, harbouring anchors.

I feel a kinship so I'm

interested in your remote memoirs,
drawn to marooned narratives
that are thirsting to be told
by back-when storykeepers.

You know the ones, they

meander up a stone staircase,
whisper lore into rustling grass,
nudge napping tales with salt water breezes,
divulging bottled messages sunk into empty spaces.

As stones study stones

Venus Gate, Rocktoberfest 2011

I
am
able
to see
firsthand
the handiwork
of harmonious hands,
as handypersons skillfully
dry stack stones. I stand in awe
as they handpick, handle, figure,
chisel, fit, and most handily
construct a handcrafted
teardrop view.

Winterstone

Swoon -

calling

mystical, magical, whimsical

into rising; looping, slumping,

showcasing white-coated stories allusive,

supporting orange-dotted frivolity.

Animated mirroring lake,

reflecting playful yet wistful, asymmetrical, cylindrical

- SCULPTURE -

cylindrical, asymmetrical,

wistful yet playful.

Reflecting lake,

mirroring animated frivolity dotted orange,

supporting allusive stories coated white,

showcasing slumping, looping, rising

into whimsical, magical, mystical calling -

Swoon.

Xeriscaping

"We never know the worth of water till the well is dry."
– Thomas Fuller

It's a sultry midsummer day,
when I find a bluestone walkway,
burning and thirsting to unearth,
a landscape wise to water's worth.

I follow it to a backyard,
a resourceful picture postcard,
starring a dry-stone riverbed,
plugging the big picture ahead.

It's a scene where shorter showers,
leaves water for native flowers,
shading a stone island bee bath,
beside a wind-breaking hedged path.

I stand by a stone bench that knows,
how deep-rooted trees need to grow,
and that smallish turf is ample,
for running futures to trample.

It's a milestone moment for me,
flowing with fluid clarity:
the rightness of ceding to Earth,
a landscape wise to water's worth.

Patricia Poriz

Yore: Áísínai'pi

Your stories on stone,

picture-written engravings,

red ochre paintings.

Yukon Lazulite

winter ice
below   and
Far   snow,

dazzling
azure
glass-flower
sprays,
arranged
in
siderite   vases,
augelite   crystal
quartz

await warmth's revealing rays, to display their

gorgeously
effulgent
mineral
solitaires.

Zed

Recently I discovered zed stones and decided to compose a piece about them, so I travelled through the internet gathering information. Did you know that jewellers fashion zed stone necklaces with different coloured stones such as red, green, pink and yellow? My favourite was a blue stone necklace I found in an online catalogue; I liked it so much I may write a cheque and purchase it.

Reading that zed stone jewellery is purported to have healing powers got me to thinking about how words also have the potential to heal. That's how my mind works; it takes in one piece of information and spontaneously zigzags off in another direction. So instead of formulating a piece about zed stones, I am now zeroing in on words, and in particular, how zed words might heal a hurting nation.

Speaking of words, if you want to add some zing to my life, put on your parka, do up the zipper, and zoom over to your nearest bookstore to buy me a dictionary. I'm serious. I'd really appreciate a new dictionary or two. I find them fascinating. In my life, word mining is a labour of love and the moment I uncover a word that is new to me, there is an inner glee that oddly enough is inadequate to describe with words.

Yet in all candour, despite their merits dictionaries have their imperfections. While I don't want to belabour the point, I personally think the "S" section is a tad zazzy. By the time I get through what seems like zillions and zillions of S words, I am ready to zizz. On the other hand, the "Z" section is much too sparse and lacks zing. Shouldn't dictionary creators be zealous about saving the best for last?

I am especially perplexed by the lack of words in my dictionary beginning with the letters z-e-d. Sure there's zed, but that's about it. Looking elsewhere, I did find a small number of words that I would like to see come alongside zed in the dictionary. In particular, zedoary really grabbed my attention. More on that later.

According to the online Etymology Dictionary, the word zed is a noun meaning weapon because of the shape of the letter z in Ancient Hebrew.[5] A weapon! Why not make zed a weapon for good? Just imagine uniting Canada one zed at a time. We should start with our educational system. Zoodikers! Think how great it would be if a Canadian teacher stood in front of a classroom of possible zed-zealots and taught them to spell words that actually started with z-e-d. That might be the zenith of their academic experience. Now if only we could craft some zed words to pass on to educators. Sounds easy, right? Wrong! To prove my point, favoured ones, take a look at a few of the zed words I created.

1. **zedU**: a zippy response to an annoying American. (I'm not saying Americans are always annoying, but they are human so at some point an American is going to annoy you and it's best to be prepared.)

   example: *ZedU! We spell the same word with more letters than you do. Uh-huh, so there! Excuse my fervour neighbour, but your behaviour is not doing you any favours.*

Hmmm. When you analyse that dialogue, it appears to have a smouldering odour of rancour and could be gauged as impolite and thus un-Canadian. In my own defence, I do not have an axe to grind nor do I harbour ill will to those who live in the centre of North America. I was simply trying to mould a new word, and fuelled by my zest to create a zed word, I seem to have constructed a zedbomb. So while inside you may be clamouring to lob a zedU at an American, remember it might be labelled as zabernism.

2. **zedzee**: the argument that "z" should be pronounced zed not zee, as in, for example, the ABC song. Just look in the dictionary, zed comes before zee. Could it be any clearer?

   example: *The zedzee principle shows you've been misled, so won't you please say zed instead?* (Note the Canadian civility.)

Initially I thought this sounded cordial, but now I'm zithering about it. (I know zithering isn't an actual word, but I like it.) So what do you think? Is zedzee affable or does it have a lustre of haughtiness, or worse still, zoilism, and therefore might erroneously be utilized for pummelling?

I'm feeling fretful, so give me a minute. I think I need to sit in the shade of my arbour and sway to the zydeco tunes playing on my Bluetooth. Yes, that's better.

Now that I'm relaxed, I am able to focus once again on the potential of zed. In actuality, Canada is a very diverse nation which unfortunately can result in misunderstandings and fear, which are such injurious emotions. I recommend that to heal, and to prevent further hurts, what we need is a common denominator. Canadian citizens are all expected to pronounce "z" as zed so why not employ zed as the common thread that ties everyone together by creating uniquely Canadian zed words that reflect our myriad of backgrounds and languages? As a bonus, just imagine all the zed words this might add to the "Z" section of the dictionary. At the very least, perhaps someone will publish a Canadian zine devoted to zed. Zounds!

Earlier I mentioned zedoary. I would now like to propose that as part of the Zed Project, zedoary be named Canada's national spice. Why? Well, the obvious answer would be because it starts with z-e-d. But did you know that zedoary can be made into a paste that aids in the healing process? It's like a zedbalm! Isn't that marvellous?

Also, for those of you who are truly committed to embracing zed, may I suggest a trip to Zedea where you can view a few khachkars or Armenian cross-stones? If you prefer staying in Canada, why not enjoy a night or two in a Hotel Zed?

Yes, zed words are my cause and I'm committed! I have to admit, nevertheless, that sitting for aeons and aeons in my pajamas, in my parlour, trying to forge zed words while noshing on an assortment of ziti, zwieback and zeppola is a truly gruelling endeavour, but that does not give me licence to quit. No, no! A high calibre manoeuvre such as the Zed Project has too much potential to be cancelled; thus, I will savour any challenge and with valour move forward. (I know what you are thinking, and no, I do not have a background in the theatre, but I will admit I may be a trifle zonked on the possibilities of zed.)

Now, no more dithering (I still prefer zithering) on your part. Please tell me, will you put on a red-maple-leaf-covered-zoot suit and join me on the Zed Project? I know this all sounds a tad zany, but as people of vigour let's add some flavour to our vocabulary and honour the zed-zone. Come on Canada, humour me!

Patricia Poriz (spelt p, o, r, i, zed)

Endnotes

[1] *"Here Lies." Being a Collection of Ancient and Modern, Humorous and Queer Inscriptions from Tombstones.* (1901). W.H. Howe. New York: New Amsterdam Book Company, Anno Domino. (p. 67).

[2] *Ice: The Nature, the History, and the Uses of an Astonishing Substance.* (2005). Mariana Gosnell. New York: Alfred A. Knopf. (pp. 418-420).

[3] *Stonechat (Saxicola torquata) in New Brunswick – first record for North America.* (1986, Spring). James G. Wilson. American Birds. 40(1), pp. 16-17. https://sora.unm.edu/node/210

[4] *Jane Eyre.* (n.d.). Charlotte Brontë. Dean & Son Ltd. London.

[5] http://www.etymonline.com/index.php?term=zed

Photograph List

Oldefar:

1. Arthur Biggerton Critchfield. (1872-1981). Family Collection.

Underpinning:

1. Charles Rueben Ritchie. (1891-1962). Family Collection.

The Strength of Stones:

1. Hillcrest/Riverbottom train station. Crowsnest Museum & Archives.

2. Ellen (Nellie) Ritchie and sons Charlie & George. Family Collection.

3. Charles, George, Betty, Allan, Ellen & Charlie Ritchie. Family Collection.

4. Ellen Ritchie and grandson Allan G. Ritchie. Family Collection.

5. Ritchie house on Dairy Road. Family Collection.

6. Ellen Agnes (Keen) Ritchie. (1897-1969). Family Collection.

Agita:

1. Frank Slide. Crowsnest Museum & Archives, Gushul Collection 03658.

Carved in Stone:

1. Procession to Bellevue Union Cemetery. Crowsnest Museum & Archives, Gushul Collection 00131.

2. Bellevue Union Cemetery. "Danysh." John Kinnear, photographer.

3. Bellevue Union Cemetery. "Notch." John Kinnear, photographer.

Stepping Stones:

1. Passburg Union Cemetery. Family Collection.

2. Karen Marie Ritchie. (1964-1977). Family Collection.

Full Circle:

1. Carousel, Jackie's Burger Bar, and Ann's Service Station. 1972. Martin Family Collection.

2. Carousel. 1972. Martin Family Collection.

The Wayside Chapel:

1. The Little Church / Wayside Chapel. Crowsnest Museum & Archives.

Still and All

1. Laurel Hill Cemetery. 2008. Kirsten Pries, photographer. Heritage Resources Centre (Uof Waterloo), Historic Resources Initiative.

In Memory:

1. Front: Karen Ritchie, Alfred Jensen, Patricia Ritchie. Back: Barbara & Debra Ritchie. Family Collection.

2. Karen Ritchie. Family Collection.

3. From right: LaRue (Jensen) Ritchie, Patricia, Barbara, Debra & Karen Ritchie. Family Collection.

4. Karen, Allan, LaRue & Gary Ritchie. Family Collection.

Reading List

Alberta Stonecat Recovery Plan 2013-2023. (2014). Government of Alberta - Alberta Species at Risk Recovery Plan No. 33.

All About Birds. Online Guide to Birds and Bird Watching. The Cornell Lab of Ornithology. https://www.allaboutbirds.org/

Ancient Uses of Ramah Chert. (2002). Kevin McAleese. Heritage Newfoundland & Labrador. http://www.heritage.nf.ca/

Canadian Cities With Most Uncomfortable Temperatures. Liz Osborn. https://www.currentresults.com/index.php

Canoeing expedition on the Keele River in the Northwest Territories. The Great Canadian Adventure Company. https://adventures.com/

Changes could be coming to Carters Beach. (2017, Sept 30). Barb McKenna. Queens County Advance. http://www.theadvance.ca/

Chimney Trail. eh Canada. https://www.ehcanadatravel.com/

Church and Nature Trust Strike Historic Partnership. (2010, Dec). Ana Watts. The New Brunswick Anglican. http://fredericton.anglican.org/nb_ang.html

Dan, Dan the Weatherman's Canadian Weather Trivia Page. http://www.dandantheweatherman.com/cantriv.html

Death Valley's moving rock mystery finally cracked. (2014, Aug 28). Rob Quinn. USA Today. https://www.usatoday.com/

Emblems and Symbols. Yukon Government. http://www.gov.yk.ca/

Extinct bird immortalized in N.L. (2010, Aug 08). CBC News. http://www.cbc.ca/news

Fort St. John Native Brock Jellison Recaps Olympic Opening Ceremonies Performance. (2010, Feb 18). NHUSER. https://energeticcity.ca/

From Montreal to Ottawa. (2012, Sept 02). SR. Mary-Louise PDDM. Pilgrim Progress – a disciple on a journey! http://pilgrimsprogresspddm.blogspot.ca/

Funk Island Valleyfield, Newfoundland. IBA Canada. http://www.ibacanada.org/

Going the distance for the piping plover. (2015, March 12). Staff Writer. Conservator. http://www.conservator.ca/

Great Auk. The Canadian Encyclopedia. http://www.thecanadianencyclopedia.ca/en/

Great Wall of Saskatchewan. (1998). 22(2) p.21. (Update 2017, Dec 07). Farm Show. https://www.farmshow.com/

Grindstone Island Conservation Easement. Nature Trust of New Brunswick. http://www.naturetrust.nb.ca/wp/

Grindstone Island: Quaker Peace Education Centre. Quakers in the World. http://www.quakersintheworld.org/

Groundhog Day: Top 11 Groundhogs to Watch (Photos). (2010, Jan 26). The Weather Channel. https://weather.com/

Hail to Thee. Weather Almanac for July 2002. The Weather Doctor. http://www.islandnet.com/~see/weather/almanac/arc2002/alm-02jul.htm

Harlequin Duck, Histrionicus histrionicus. Canada's Arctic. http://www.arctic.uoguelph.ca/cpl/organisms/birds/marine/ducks/harlequin.htm

Harlequin Duck in New Brunswick. New Brunswick Museum. http://www.nbm-mnb.ca/index.php/component/content/article?id=308

"Here Lies." Being a Collection of Ancient and Modern, Humorous and Queer Inscriptions from Tombstones. (1901). W.H. Howe. New Amsterdam Book Company, Anno Domino. (p. 67). https://archive.org/details/hereliesbeingac00howegoog

Ice: The Nature, the History, and the Uses of an Astonishing Substance. (2005). Mariana Gosnell. New York: Alfred A. Knopf.

Induction Showcase. Bill McCreary – Referee/Linesman Category. The Official Site of the Hockey Hall of Fame. http://www.hhof.com/index.html

In our own backyard: Rigaud shrine offers visitors a tranquil setting. (2009, June 18). Kristina Edson. Montreal Gazette. Retrieved from https://www.pressreader.com/canada/montreal-gazette/20090618/282312496047693

Is Peyto Lake Really That Blue? [Audrey, Blog post]. Banff and Beyond. http://banffandbeyond.com/

Jane Eyre. (n.d.). Charlotte Brontë. Dean & Son Ltd. London.

Keele River. Canoe North Adventures. http://canoenorthadventures.com/

Kerry Fraser. Voted Best NHL Referee, Author, Analyst on C'mon Ref and TSN. Keynote Speakers Canada. http://keynotespeakerscanada.ca/

Kitjigattalik – The Ramah Chert Quarries, Torngat Mountain National Park, Newfoundland and Labrador. (2016, Feb 15). Government of Canada. https://www.canada.ca/en/parks-canada.html

Laurel Hill Cemetery. Canada's Historic Places. http://www.historic-places.ca/

Lazulite with Siderite, Quartz and Apatite. (2012, April 19). Mineral Auctions. https://www.mineralauctions.com/

Linda Parker Hamilton. The Northern Nightingale. http://www.northernnightingale.com/index.html

Little Limestone Lake. CPAWS Manitoba Chapter. http://cpawsmb.org/campaigns/little-limestone-lake

Little Limestone Lake Park Reserve. Government of Manitoba. http://www.gov.mb.ca/sd/pai/mb_network/little_limestone/

Living Among the Stone Sheep of Todagin Mountain. Global Wildlife Conservation. https://www.globalwildlife.org/

Looking for the Stones of Stones Cove. (2014, July 27). [Tony, Blog post]. My Newfoundland Kayak Experience. http://mynewfoundlandkayakexperience.blogspot.ca/

Longest whistling marathon. Jennifer Anavi Davies. (2010, Oct 03). Guinness World Records. http://www.guinnessworldrecords.com/

Meet Carol Huynh, Canada's First Olympic Women's Wrestling Champion. (2015, Mar 05). https://www.olympic.org/

Mementos. Charlotte Brontë. http://digital.library.upenn.edu/women/bronte/poems/pbc-mementos.html

My Little Blue Story Book. Revised Edition. (1964). Odille Ousley and David H. Russell. The Ginn Basic Readers. Ginn and Company.

No Stone Left Alone Memorial Foundation. https://www.nostoneleftalone.ca/about-nsla/

PEI's Oldest Object. Spearpoint donated to PEI Museum & Heritage Foundation. The BUZZ. https://www.buzzon.com/index.php/news-articles/community/14923-peis-oldest-object

Piping plover (Charadrius melodus). Wildlife Preservation Canada. https://wildlifepreservation.ca/piping-plover/

Prince Edward Island's Oldest Artefact. (2016, June). Jack Sorensen. Tyron and Area Historical Society Newsletter. https://tryonareahistoricalsociety.com/

Quebec's Magical Magdelens. (2010, Nov 16). Cherie Thiessen. Twitter Stuff. http://cthiessen.com/

Resolute Bay | Qausuittuq. Nunavut Inuit Wildlife Secretariat http://www.niws.ca/baffin-north-communities/resolute-bay-qausuittuq/

Robert Homme (1919-2002). History of Canadian Broadcasting. https://broadcasting-history.ca/

Rock Art Preservation. (2017, July 04). Writing-on-Stone Provincial Park. Alberta Parks. https://www.albertaparks.ca/

Rock Art. (2014, April). Park Notes. Alberta Parks. https://www.albertaparks.ca/media/6494252/writing-on-stone-pp-rock-art-park-notes.pdf

Rocky Mountain House National Historic Site. Parks Canada. https://www.pc.gc.ca/en

Rocky Mountain House National Historic Site. eh Canada. https://www.ehcanadatravel.com/

Sedum lanceolatum. EOL Encyclopedia of Life http://eol.org/

Springtime Stoneflies. Bill Robertson. The Fishing Hole. Angler's Post. http://social.thefishinhole.com/

Stonecat (Noturus flavus). BioKids. http://www.biokids.umich.edu/

Stonechat (Saxicola torquata) in New Brunswick – first record for North America. (1986, Spring). James G. Wilson. American Birds. 40(1), pp. 16-17. https://sora.unm.edu/node/210

Stonecrop (Sedum Spp.) Northern Bushcraft. Wild Edible Plants. http://northernbushcraft.com/

Stoneflies (Golden Stone Fly Adult). Alpine Anglers. Articles. http://www.alpineanglers.com/

Stonefly Family Perlidae (Golden Stones). Troutnut. http://www.troutnut.com/

Stone's Sheep of the Northern Rockies: The Effects of Access. (1999, March). M.M. Paquet and R.A. Demarchi. Foundation for North American Wild Sheep (FNAWS) and Guide-Outfitters Association of British Columbia (GOABC). http://www.env.gov.bc.ca/wld/documents/stonessheep/stonesheep_1.pdf

Stone's Sheep Trail Hike. Muncho Lake Provincial Park. (2016, Sept 03). Trip 117. ihikebc. http://ihikebc.com/

Stories by the Qqlliq. Brittany Holliss [Blog post]. Museum of Inuit Art Blog. https://museumofinuitartblog.wordpress.com/tag/oil-lamp/

The Crowsnest River. (2017, April 20). Dave Brown Outfitters. http://davebrownoutfitters.com/the-crowsnest-river/

The Dry Stone Venus Gate Amphitheatre, Canada. Natural Homes. http://naturalhomes.org/timeline/drystone-amphitheatre.htm

The Great Auk – Canada's Penguin. Danny Catt. Catt-Trax 2. https://commons.bcit.ca/catttrax2/node/435/index.html

Thinhorn Sheep in British Columbia. (2000). British Columbia Ministry of Environment, Lands and Parks. http://www.env.gov.bc.ca/wld/documents/thinhorn.pdf

Thirty-One Hours on Grindstone Island: The Canadian and American Friends Service Committees' Experiment in Civil Defence. (2006). Robynne Rogers Healey, PhD. Canadian Quaker History Journal. 71, pp. 22-32. http://cfha.info/journal71p22.pdf

Top 10 Incredible Lakes in Canada. PandoTrip. Places in North America. https://www.pandotrip.com/

Tournament of Beaches: Day Two. (2012, Aug 01). Melissa Leong. National Post. http://nationalpost.com/

Types of Poetry. Shadow Poetry. http://www.shadowpoetry.com/

"Ulus" and Spearpoints. Two New Archaeological Finds From Prince Edward Island. (1984). David L. Keenlyside. The Island Magazine. http://vre2.upei.ca/islandmagazine/

Uncovering Tragedy at the old Bellevue Cemetery. (2013, June 25). John Kinnear. Crowsnest Pass Herald. 83(25). http://passherald.ca/

Yukon Phosphates, Lazulite, Rapid Creek, Yukon Territory, Item #1224 Lazulite. David K. Joyce Minerals. http://www.davidkjoyceminerals.com/pagefiles/specimen_gallery. asp?TitleID=322&refpage=minerals

What was the greatest single-day temperature change in Canadian history?
https://www.theweathernetwork.com/ca

What We Do Together That We Can't Do Alone (02. Jaime Angelopolous (Toronto), Swoon). (2016). CAFKA. https://www.cafka.org/

When the Last of the Great Auks Died, It Was by the Crush of a Fisherman's Boot. (2014, July 10). Samantha Galasso. Smithsonian Magazine. https://www.smithsonianmag.com/

In Memory
Karen Marie Ritchie

"...set time heartbreakingly brief, but grief's
mustard seed faith believed, not lost but gone before."